BIRTH

Full name at birth:_____

Date of birth:_____

place photo here

Height/Weight:_____

Place of birth:_____

Parents names:_____

I was named after: _____

President :_____

Average price for a home:_____

Average annual income:_____

Gallon of gas:_____

Gallon of milk:_____

Dozen eggs:_____

page 1

Siblings names and birthdates:
_____
_____
_____
_____
_____

When I was a baby, my parents described me as.....
_____
_____
_____
_____
_____
_____
_____
_____

\

TODDLER

Place photo here

I first learned to walk :

_____

_____

My first words were :

_____

_____

I quit wearing diapers at age..

_____

_____

I first learned to count at age..

_____

_____

CHILDHOOD

Nickname:_____

_____

I grew up in: _____

_____

_____

My favorite childhood memory:_____

_____

_____

_____

_____

_____

_____

_____

_____

CHILDHOOD

My best friend from childhood was:

_____

_____

_____

_____

_____

_____

miss this most about my childhood:

_____

_____

_____

_____

_____

_____

_____

CHILDHOOD

Add photos here

CHILDHOOD

Add photos here

CHILDHOOD

Some of my favorite TV shows were:

_____

_____

_____

_____

Some of my favorite toys were:

_____

_____

_____

_____

_____

_____

_____

My favorite song/s were:

_____

_____

_____

CHILDHOOD

I played these sports:

_____

_____

_____

_____

This was the first sporting event I went to:

_____

_____

_____

_____

_____

_____

_____

_____

_____

_____

CHILDHOOD

This is who I looked up to most and why:

CHILDHOOD

Some of my favorite foods, candys, drinks ect were:

_____

_____

_____

_____

_____

_____

I started to cook at this age.. and this is what I cooked first:

_____

_____

_____

_____

_____

_____

_____

_____

CHILDHOOD

This is what my parents would prepare for meals:

ADOLESCENCE

This is how I dressed and styled my hair:

_____

_____

_____

_____

_____

_____

This is how many friends I had:

_____

_____

_____

_____

_____

_____

ADOLESCENCE

Add photos here

ADOLESCENCE

Add photos here

ADOLESCENCE

The genre of music I liked:

_____

_____

What was popular at the time:

_____

_____

My favorite bands/artists were:

_____

_____

_____

_____

My first concert ever was:

_____

_____

_____

ADOLESCENCE

These are the sports I played:

_____

_____

_____

My hobbies were:

_____

_____

_____

_____

_____

_____

_____

_____

_____

_____

ADOLESCENCE

This is how I spent my weekends:

_____
_____
_____
_____
_____
_____
_____
_____
_____
_____
_____
_____
_____
_____
_____
_____

ADOLESCENCE

My dating life in highschool:

_____
_____
_____
_____
_____
_____
_____
_____
_____
_____

I went to prom with:

_____
_____
_____
_____
_____

ADOLESCENCE

I learned to drive when:

_____
_____
_____
_____
_____
_____
_____
_____
_____
_____
_____
_____
_____
_____
_____
_____

ADOLESCENCE

I first learned to drive in this car:

_____

_____

_____

_____

_____

_____

My very first car was:

_____

_____

_____

My dream car at the time was:

_____

_____

_____

_____

ADOLESCENCE

These are the kinds of grades I got:

___

___

___

___

My most and least favorite subjects :

___

___

___

___

___

___

___

___

___

ADOLESCENCE

My favorite teachers:

ADOLESCENCE

This was my very first job and this is how much I made:

_____
_____
_____
_____
_____
_____

This was my dream job:

_____
_____
_____
_____
_____
_____
_____

ADOLESCENCE

This was my highschool and the year I graduated:

_____

_____

_____

The advice I would give my teenage self now, and what I would change:

_____

_____

_____

_____

_____

_____

_____

_____

_____

_____

_____

_____

FAMILY

My Mother's maiden name was:

_____

My relationship with my Mother was like this:

_____

_____

_____

_____

_____

_____

_____

_____

_____

_____

_____

_____

_____

FAMILY

My relationship with my Father was like this:

_____

_____

_____

_____

_____

_____

_____

_____

_____

_____

_____

_____

_____

_____

_____

FAMILY

Add photos here

FAMILY

Add photos here

FAMILY

This is how my parents met:

_____
_____
_____
_____
_____
_____
_____
_____
_____
_____
_____
_____
_____
_____
_____
_____
_____

FAMILY

My relationship with my siblings was like this:

FAMILY

This is how I'm similar and different from my family:

FAMILY

These are the unique gifts and talents that my parents had:

_____

_____

_____

_____

_____

_____

_____

_____

_____

_____

_____

_____

_____

_____

_____

FAMILY

Family traditions that were passed to me:

What I do better than anyone else in my family:

FAMILY

The best advice my parents gave me:

FAMILY

My favorite memory of my Mother:

_____

_____

_____

_____

_____

_____

_____

_____

_____

_____

_____

_____

_____

_____

_____

FAMILY

My favorite memory of my Father:

FAMILY

My favorite memory of my Grandparents:

MOTHERHOOD

The first person I told when I found out I was pregnant/adopting:

_____

_____

_____

This is how old I was and what it was like when I became a Mother:

_____

_____

_____

_____

_____

_____

_____

The name I wanted for my child other than the one chosen:

_____

_____

_____

MOTHERHOOD

Add photos here

MOTHERHOOD

Add photos here

MOTHERHOOD

My baby's first words:

___

___

___

___

When they first learned to walk:

___

___

___

___

This is what I had to do to calm them:

___

___

___

___

___

___

___

MOTHERHOOD

The ways my child/children are similar/different than me:

_____
_____
_____
_____
_____
_____
_____
_____

Biggest difference in how kids are raised now vs. then:

_____
_____
_____
_____
_____
_____
_____

MOTHERHOOD

The things I would change about how my child/children were raised:

MOTHERHOOD

The most rewarding/challenging parts of motherhood:

___
___
___
___
___
___
___
___
___
___
___
___
___
___
___

SPIRITUALITY

How my beliefs and religious practices have changed throughout life:

_____

_____

_____

_____

_____

_____

_____

_____

_____

_____

_____

_____

_____

_____

_____

SPIRITUALITY

The beliefs or religious practices of my parents when I was growing up:

_____
_____
_____
_____
_____
_____
_____
_____
_____
_____
_____
_____
_____
_____
_____
_____
_____

SPIRITUALITY

Fate? Or free will? This is what I believe has the most influence:

_____
_____
_____
_____
_____
_____
_____

I believe the purpose of life is:

_____
_____
_____
_____
_____
_____
_____

SPIRITUALITY

Miracles and my personal beliefs about them:

_____
_____
_____
_____
_____
_____
_____
_____

This person has had the biggest spiritual influence on my life:

_____
_____
_____
_____
_____
_____
_____

CAREER

My career/s throughout life and where the inspiration came from:

CAREER

The business I've always wanted to have:

_____

_____

_____

_____

If I could have any profession in life, it would be this:

_____

_____

_____

_____

_____

_____

_____

The profession my parents wanted for me:

_____

_____

_____

CAREER

Add photos here

CAREER

Add photos here

TRAVEL

This is my favorite place to visit!

_____

_____

_____

_____

_____

_____

_____

_____

_____

My dream destination:

_____

_____

_____

_____

TRAVEL

My favorite travel memory:

TRAVEL

Add photos here

TRAVEL

Add photos here

TRAVEL

The top ten places I would like to visit and why:

_____

_____

_____

_____

_____

_____

_____

_____

_____

_____

_____

_____

_____

_____

_____

LOVE

My beliefs on soulmates:

_____
_____
_____
_____
_____
_____
_____
_____

The most important qualities in a successful relationship:

_____
_____
_____
_____
_____
_____
_____
_____

LOVE

Add photos here

LOVE

The biggest way I believe relationships have changed over the years:

_____
_____
_____
_____
_____
_____
_____
_____
_____

Love poem or song written/ dedicated to me:

_____
_____
_____
_____
_____
_____

LOVE

Advice I would share with new couples:

SELF

My daily routine, workout, diet, ect.:

___

___

___

___

___

___

My introversion/extroversion and how that's changed throughout life:

___

___

___

___

___

___

___

___

___

___

SELF

Add photos here

SELF

What I love most about myself:

_____
_____
_____
_____
_____
_____
_____

The most impulsive thing I've ever done:

_____
_____
_____
_____
_____
_____
_____
_____
_____

SELF

Some of my favorite foods now:

___

___

___

___

___

___

___

My favorite seasons:

___

___

___

___

___

___

___

___

___

SELF

My favorite holidays and why:

_____
_____
_____
_____
_____
_____
_____

My most cherished holiday memory:

_____
_____
_____
_____
_____
_____
_____
_____
_____
_____

SELF

I'm most proud of these accomplishments:

_____

_____

_____

_____

_____

_____

_____

_____

_____

_____

_____

_____

_____

_____

_____

_____

SELF

A perfect day for me would look like this:

_____
_____
_____
_____
_____
_____
_____
_____
_____
_____
_____
_____
_____
_____
_____
_____

SELF

My top ten favorite movies, TV shows, and books:

_____

_____

_____

_____

_____

_____

_____

_____

_____

_____

_____

_____

_____

_____

_____

_____

_____

_____

SELF

My favorite band/artist and how that's changed over my life:

_____
_____
_____
_____
_____
_____
_____
_____

Favorite genre of music and how that's changed over my life:

_____
_____
_____
_____
_____
_____
_____
_____

SELF

If I got to start all over at life, this is what I would change:

LEGACY

This is what I want to be remembered for:

www.ingramcontent.com/pod-product-compliance
Lightning Source LLC
Chambersburg PA
CBHW020308010526
44107CB00001B/32